To:

From:

THE NEWS

A Dog Is Your Best Friend

Compiled by Lois L. Kaufman

Illustrated by Paula Brinkman

 PETER PAUPER PRESS, INC.
WHITE PLAINS, NEW YORK

Designed by Arlene Greco

Text copyright © 2000
Peter Pauper Press, Inc.
202 Mamaroneck Avenue
White Plains, NY 10601
Illustrations copyright © 2000
Paula Brinkman
All rights reserved
ISBN 0-88088-398-7
Printed in China
7 6 5

Visit us at www.peterpauper.com

A Dog Is Your Best Friend

*D*o you suppose it's only a coincidence that man's best friend can't talk?

Anonymous

If you are a dog and
your owner suggests that
you wear a sweater . . .
suggest that he wear
a tail.

Fran Lebowitz

To his dog, every man is Napoleon; hence the constant popularity of dogs.

Aldous Huxley

Dogs are not our whole life, but they make our lives whole.

Roger Caras

*T*he most affectionate

creature in the world is

a wet dog.

Ambrose Bierce

The dog has seldom been successful in pulling man up to its level of sagacity, but man has frequently dragged the dog down to his.

James Thurber

The dog is a Yes-animal, very popular with people who can't afford to keep a Yes-man.

Robertson Davies

$\mathcal{O}$utside of a dog, a
book is probably man's
best friend, and inside of a
dog, it's too dark to read.

Groucho Marx

If you pick up a
starving dog and make
him prosperous, he
will not bite you.
This is the principal
difference between a
dog and a man.

Mark Twain

You can say any fool thing to a dog, and the dog will give you this look that says, "My God, you're RIGHT! I NEVER would've thought of that!"

Dave Barry

In order to really enjoy a dog, one doesn't merely try to train him to be semihuman. The point of it is to open oneself to the possibility of becoming partly a dog.

Edward Hoagland

Things that upset a terrier may pass virtually unnoticed by the Great Dane.

Dr. Smiley Blanton

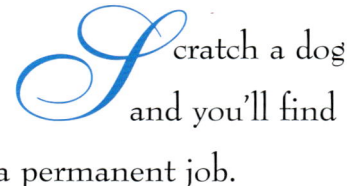

*S*cratch a dog
and you'll find
a permanent job.

Franklin P. Jones

The great pleasure of a dog is that you make a fool of yourself with him and not only will he not scold you, but he will make a fool of himself too.

Samuel Butler

You can talk to a dog all day long, but he's just looking at you and thinking, "Where's the ball?"

Mike Myers

If dogs could talk it
would take a lot of
the fun out of
owning one.

Andrew A. Rooney

I play a lot with my dogs, keep their love for me intact. We . . . have three. I'm a homebody.

Noah Wyle

A well-trained dog will make no attempt to share your lunch. He will just make you feel so guilty that you cannot enjoy it.

Helen Thomson

I once decided not to date a guy because he wasn't excited to meet my dog. I mean, this was like not wanting to meet my mother.

Bonnie Schacter

Dogs are truly happy to see you. They don't wish you empty things like "Hey, have a nice day." They embrace you as the essence of their nice day.

Phil Reisman

I've seen a look in dogs' eyes, a quickly vanishing look of amazed contempt, and I am convinced that basically dogs think humans are nuts.

John Steinbeck

Dogs, the foremost snobs
in creation, are quick to
notice the difference
between a well-clad and a
disreputable stranger.

Albert Payson Terhune

Old dogs, like old shoes, are comfortable. They might be a bit out of shape and a little worn around the edges, but they fit well.

Bonnie Wilcox

If a dog will not come
to you after having
looked you in the face,
you should go home
and examine your
conscience.

Woodrow Wilson

Animals are such agreeable friends—they ask no questions, they pass no criticisms.

George Eliot

*W*hen a man's best friend is his dog, that dog has a problem.

Edward Abbey

You may have a dog that won't sit up, roll over or even cook breakfast, not because she's too stupid to learn how but because she's too smart to bother.

Rick Horowitz,
Chicago Tribune

[Dogs] never talk about themselves but listen to you while you talk about yourself, and keep up an appearance of being interested in the conversation.

Jerome K. Jerome

I like a bit of a
mongrel myself, whether
it's a man or a dog;
they're the best for
every day.

George Bernard Shaw

No one appreciates
the very special
genius of your
conversation as
the dog does.

Christopher Morley

Did you ever walk into a room and forget why you walked in? I think that is how dogs spend their lives.

Sue Murphy

If you eliminate smoking
and gambling, you
will be amazed to find
that almost all an
Englishman's pleasures
can be, and mostly are,
shared by his dog.

George Bernard Shaw

[Dogs] know exactly what makes them happy—doing something for someone. They will do everything they can think of to please their human companion, and any signs that they have been successful make them very happy.

John Richard Stephens

Humankind is drawn to dogs because they are so like ourselves—bumbling, affectionate, confused, easily disappointed, eager to be amused, grateful for kindness and the least attention.

Pam Brown

People are meant to go through the world two by two. I want someone to share my life with, to do errands with, for companionship. I'm not particularly preoccupied with the husband-baby thing. It's not a driving force for me right now because my life is really full. I have a dog.

Calista Flockhart

A dog teaches a boy fidelity, perseverance, and to turn around three times before lying down.

Robert Benchley

In the whole history of
the world there is but
one thing that money
cannot buy—the wag
of a dog's tail.

Henry Wheeler Shaw ("Josh Billings")

When a man's dog turns
against him, it is time for
a wife to pack her trunk
and go home to mama.

Mark Twain

Dogs, bless them, operate on the premise that human beings are fragile and require incessant applications of affection and reassurance. The random lick of the hand and the furry chin draped over the instep are calculated to let the shaky owner know that a friend is nearby.

Mary McGrory

A barking dog is often more useful than a sleeping lion.

Washington Irving

*E*xtraordinary creature!
So close a friend, and
yet so remote.

Thomas Mann

Since I have taken to sleeping under the bed, I have come to know tranquility I never imagined possible. You never really know when it might be cookie time. And that's what the dogs have taught me.

Merrill Markoe

The biggest
dog has been
a pup.

Joaquin Miller

I think dogs are the most amazing creatures; they give unconditional love. For me they are the role model for being alive.

Gilda Radner

If I have any beliefs about immortality, it is that certain dogs I have known will go to heaven, and very, very few persons.

James Thurber

I have found that when you are deeply troubled there are things you get from the silent devoted companionship of a dog that you can get from no other source.

Doris Day

The dog was created especially for children. He is the god of frolic.

Henry Ward Beecher

Were my Maker to grant me but one single glance through these sightless eyes of mine . . . I would without question or recall choose to see first a child, then a dog.

Helen Keller

Buy a pup and your
money will buy love
unflinching.

Rudyard Kipling

The more I see of the representatives of the people, the more I admire my dogs.

Alphonse de Lamartine

The censure of a dog is something no man can stand.

Christopher Morley

Down in the silent hallway
  Scampers the dog about,
And whines, and barks,
and scratches,
  In order to get out.

Once in the glittering starlight,
  He straightway doth begin
To set up a doleful howling
  In order to get in.

Richard Kendall Munkittrick

He cannot be a gentleman
which loveth not a dog.

John Northbrooke

Histories are more full of examples of the fidelity of dogs than of friends.

Alexander Pope

Our dogs will love and admire the meanest of us, and feed our colossal vanity with their uncritical homage.

Agnes Repplier

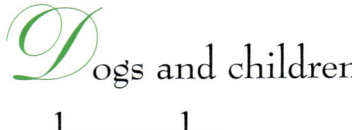

Dogs and children
know who
likes them.

Proverb

I have a dog of Blenheim birth,

With fine long ears and full

   of mirth;

And sometimes, running

   o'er the plain,

   He tumbles on his nose:

But quickly jumping up again

   Like lightning on he goes!

John Ruskin

$\mathcal{W}$ho loves me will
love my dog also.

St. Bernard of Clairvaux

No man is so poor that he can't afford to keep one dog, and I've seen them so poor they could afford to keep three.

Henry Wheeler Shaw ("Josh Billings")

It often happens that a man is more humanely related to a cat or dog than to any human being.

Henry David Thoreau

A dog, I will maintain,
is a very tolerable judge
of beauty, as appears
from the fact that any
liberally educated dog
does, in a general way,
prefer a woman to a
man.

Francis Thompson

$\mathcal{D}$ogs laugh, but they laugh with their tails.

Max Eastman

The one absolutely
unselfish friend that man
can have in this selfish
world, the one that never
deserts him, the one that
never proves ungrateful or
treacherous, is his dog. . . .
When all other friends
desert, he remains.

George Graham Vest,
Speech in the Senate, 1884

The possession of a dog today is a different thing from the possession of a dog at the turn of the century, when one's dog was fed on mashed potato and brown gravy and lived in a dog-house with an arched portal. Today a dog is fed on scraped beef and Vitamin B1, and lives in bed with you.

E. B. White

Bark: This is a sound made by dogs when excited. Dogs bark at milkmen, postmen, yourself, visitors to the house and other dogs; some of them bark at nothing. For some reason dogs tend not to bark at burglars, bailiffs and income tax collectors, at whom they wag their tails in the most friendly manner.

Geoffrey Williams

Our German forefathers
had a very kind religion.
They believed that, after
death, they would meet
again all the good dogs
that had been their com-
panions in life. I wish I
could believe that, too.

Otto von Bismarck

EPITAPH FOR HIS DOG
BURIED AT NEWSTEAD ABBEY, 1808

Near this spot

Are deposited the remains of one

Who possessed beauty without vanity,

Strength without insolence,

Courage without ferocity,

And all the virtues of man without his vices.

This praise, which would be unmeaning flattery

If inscribed over human ashes,

Is but a just tribute to the memory of

Boatswain, a dog.

Lord Byron